Dwyane Wade

by Michael Sandler

Consultant: Charlie Zegers
Basketball Expert
basketball.about.com

New York, New York

Credits

Cover and Title Page, © Victor Baldizon/NBAE via Getty Images, Jeff Schear/WireImage/Getty Images, and Jeff Schear/WireImage for Wade's World Foundation/Getty Images; 4, © Mike Ehrmann/Getty Images; 5, © AP Photo/Nam Y. Huh; 6, © AP Photo/David J. Phillip; 7, © Jeff Schear/WireImage for Wade's World Foundation/Getty Images; 8, © Tim Loftus; 9, © AP Photo/ Charlie Neibergall; 10, © John Gress/Reuters/Landov; 11, © Lucy Nicholson/Reuters/Landov; 12, © Jeff Schear; 13, © Jeff Schear; 14, © Jeff Schear/WireImage/Getty Images; 15, © Jeff Schear/ WireImage for Wade's World Foundation/Getty Images; 16, © Jeff Schear; 17, © Jeff Schear; 19, © Issac Baldizon/NBAE via Getty Images; 20, © Alexander Tamargo/Getty Images; 21, © Filippo Monteforte/AFP/Getty Images; 22R, © AP Photo/Tom DiPace; 22L, © MCT/Newscom.

Publisher: Kenn Goin
Senior Editor: Lisa Wiseman
Creative Director: Spencer Brinker
Photo Researcher: We Research Pictures, LLC

Library of Congress Cataloging-in-Publication Data

Sandler, Michael, 1965-
    Dwyane Wade / by Michael Sandler ; consultant, Charlie Zegers.
        p. cm. — (Basketball heroes making a difference)
    Includes bibliographical references and index.
    ISBN-13: 978-1-61772-441-1 (library binding)
    ISBN-10: 1-61772-441-6 (library binding)
    1. Wade, Dwyane, 1982—Juvenile literature. 2. Basketball players—United States—Biography—Juvenile literature. 3. African American basketball players—Biography—Juvenile literature. 4. Generosity—Juvenile literature. I. Zegers, Charlie. II. Title.
    GV884.W23S26 2012
    796.323092—dc23
    [B]

2011039986

For more information, write to Bearport Publishing Company, Inc., 45 West 21st Street, Suite 3B, New York, New York 10010. Printed in the United States of America.

10 9 8 7 6 5 4 3 2 1

03166 6975

Contents

Fantastic Finish

With just over three minutes left in Game 5 of the 2010–2011 **Eastern Conference** Finals, the Miami Heat was down by 12 points against the Chicago Bulls. A bad loss in such an important game seemed certain. Then Dwyane Wade showed why he is the NBA's greatest **clutch** player.

First, the six-foot-four (1.93-m) **guard** hit a smooth little **runner**. Then he drove into the **lane** for a **layup**. Next he stepped back at the three-point line and hoisted up a shot. The ball soared through the air and swished through the basket. Score! Even better for Miami, Dwyane was **fouled** while shooting. The foul sent him to the **free throw line**, where he coolly sank the ball to complete a rare **four-point play**! With some added help from teammates LeBron James and Chris Bosh, Dwyane and Miami had an 83–80 **comeback** win.

Dwyane (#3) tries to dribble past Chicago's Derrick Rose (#1) during Game 5 against the Bulls on May 26, 2011.

The Game 5 victory gave the Heat a 4–1 series win over the Bulls and earned Miami the 2010–2011 Eastern Conference Championship!

The Journey Begins

For Dwyane, the path to NBA stardom began at the age of five while growing up in Chicago, Illinois. "My father loved basketball, and he made me play. I used to like baseball and football. But he took me to the court and made me play for a week straight. I fell in love with the game," said Dwyane.

Playing the game was more fun than other parts of Dwyane's often difficult childhood. His parents separated when he was just a baby. As a young child, he lived with his mother, Jolinda, in a tough, crime-filled neighborhood. Jolinda often struggled to pay the bills. "There were no birthday presents or Christmas gifts," Dwyane said about his early childhood. "You just didn't ever ask for what you wanted."

Dwyane and his mother

Dwyane's father (left) encouraged him to play basketball at a very young age.

When he was nine years old, Dwyane moved into his father's house in Robbins, Illinois. His new neighborhood was a little safer than the one Dwyane had lived in with his mother, and he got to play lots of basketball with his three stepbrothers.

Growing Stronger

Living with just one parent was hard for Dwyane. "When I was younger, I grew up without a father. Once I got a little older, I lived with my father and I grew up without a mother," said Dwyane.

Still, with guidance from his older sister, Tragil, and his teachers in school, Dwyane grew into a confident teen. He also blossomed into a fine basketball player in high school, where he once scored more than 40 points in each of two games played on the same day!

His extraordinary basketball skills earned him a college **scholarship** to Marquette University in Milwaukee, Wisconsin. There, Dwyane became known for his unstoppable **drives** to the hoop, his unshakable confidence, and his team leadership. In his junior year, he led the Marquette Golden Eagles to their first **Final Four** appearance in more than 25 years.

As a senior, Dwyane averaged 27 points and 11 rebounds per game at Harold L. Richards High School in Oak Lawn, Illinois.

HAROLD L. RICHARDS HIGH SCHOOL

Dwyane (#3) scored 29 points, pulled down 11 rebounds, and handed out 11 assists in a 2003 victory over the University of Kentucky that sent Marquette into the Final Four.

After his junior year at Marquette, Dwyane decided to enter the 2003 NBA **draft**. The Miami Heat chose him with the draft's fifth pick.

The Man in Miami

After being drafted by the Heat, Dwyane didn't waste any time making an **impact** on the team. During his first season, he averaged 16 points a game and led Miami into the **playoffs**. He impressed fans with both his spectacular speed and his incredible spin moves to the hoop.

During the 2004–2005 season, Dwyane also impressed his teammates. Superstar Heat player Shaquille O'Neal nicknamed him "Flash" because of his strength and quickness on the court.

Dwyane and Shaq proved to be the league's greatest guard-**center** combination during the 2005–2006 season. The pair led the Heat into the NBA Finals against the Dallas Mavericks. Dallas won the first two games, but then Dwyane took over the series. He led the Heat to four straight wins and the first NBA title in Miami Heat history!

Dwyane's ever-improving play earned him a spot in the 2005 All-Star Game. Here he passes around Dallas's Dirk Nowitzki during the All-Star Game.

Dwyane (left) and Shaq (right) celebrate after winning the 2006 NBA championship.

Dwyane fought injuries after his first three seasons on the team. Still, the Heat played well and usually made the playoffs whenever Dwyane was healthy. When LeBron James and Chris Bosh joined the team for the 2010–2011 season, Dwyane led Miami back into the NBA Finals.

A Special Camp

Just a few days after celebrating Miami's first-ever NBA title in 2006, Dwyane went back to the place where he had grown up. He flew to Chicago for a very special reason: to host his annual basketball camp.

About 500 kids between the ages of 8 and 16 came to Dwyane's camp. Many were from Robbins, the suburb where Dwyane had once played ball. The campers learned basketball skills from Dwyane and other instructors, many of whom were friends or relatives of the NBA guard. The kids learned how to improve their dribbling, passing, and defense skills. Best of all, the camp was completely free for everyone, a present from Dwyane to the community where he had been raised.

"I have just as much fun as these kids," Dwyane said, shown here during his 2010 basketball camp.

Dwyane started the Dwyane Wade Basketball Camp in 2005. He has held the camp every summer since.

Wade's World

Hosting a free basketball camp is just one of the generous ways that Dwyane helps others. Another way that he helps is through the Wade's World Foundation (WWF), which he started in 2003. This **charity** has one goal: to give a helping hand to kids who are growing up in difficult situations.

Though Dwyane started the WWF as an adult, helping others is something he has thought about since he was seven years old. He remembers watching TV and seeing celebrities visit a local school. "So many kids were happy to see them. How life-changing that visit must have been," Dwyane said.

It made Dwyane wonder why no one famous or successful ever visited his neighborhood. "I decided if I ever made it, I would come back to my community and give back," he said.

Dwyane visits with students at a public school in Chicago.

Dwyane's older sister, Tragil, helped him a lot during his childhood. Today, she's helping other kids as president of the WWF.

Dwyane talks with some students at a Chicago public school.

Special Places

The WWF works extra hard in three places that are special to Dwyane: the Greater Chicago area, where he had grown up; Miami, the city where he plays basketball; and Milwaukee, the city where he had gone to college. In 2009, for example, Dwyane learned that the library in the Chicago suburb of Robbins, where he had once lived, was in danger of closing. The city didn't have enough money to keep it open. Dwyane was concerned for the kids in the town. Where would they study? Where would they get books to read? Where would they use the Internet? Not wanting the library to shut down, Dwyane jumped into action by donating $25,000 to the library, helping to keep it open.

William Leonard Public Library was able to stay open thanks to Dwyane's generous donation.

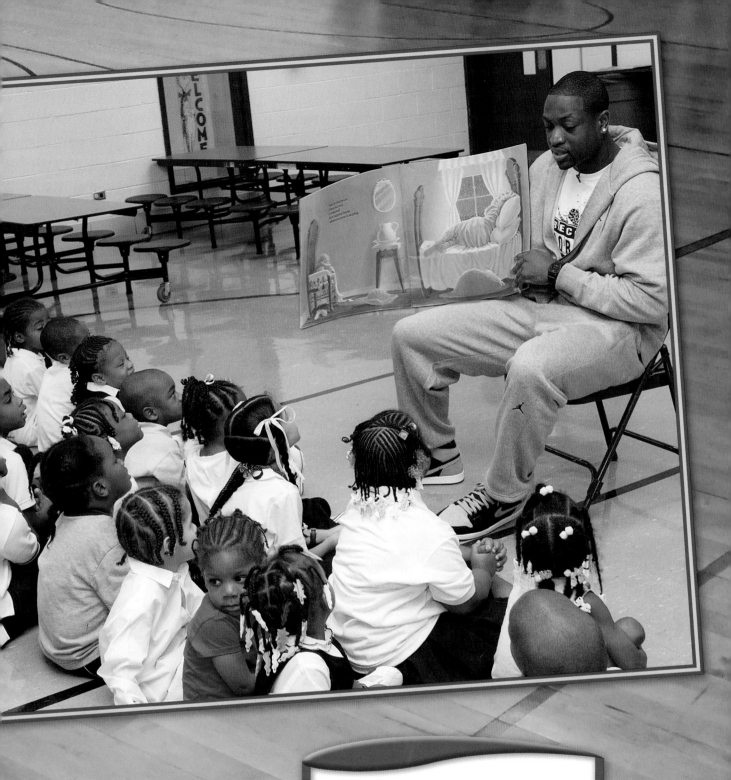

Libraries are very important to Dwyane. In September 2010, he served as Honorary Chairman of Library Card Sign-up Month, urging kids to get and use library cards.

Helping Kids and Families

In Miami, Dwyane and his foundation have helped the Miami Children's Hospital. Dwyane often visits the young patients there, bringing cheer and smiles to them. The WWF works with the hospital to raise money to improve medical care for the children it treats.

Dwyane also works with Miami charities such as Neighbors 4 Neighbors. This group helps people who are facing crises, such as losing a home in a fire. In 2010, the WWF and Neighbors 4 Neighbors worked together to pay for needy families to go on a shopping spree to buy clothing and toys. They even got to meet Dwyane.

In Milwaukee, Dwyane and the WWF have worked with the Boys & Girls Clubs of America. For the kids in this group, Dwyane holds basketball clinics and helps provide scholarships for students to attend Marquette University, where he went to school.

In 2009, Dwyane was chosen to be included in the Miami Children's Hospital Hall of Fame, which honors people who have helped to greatly improve the lives of children all over the world.

Dwyane brings a smile
to a young patient's face
during a hospital visit.

19

A True Champion

Dwyane is both a leader and a champion. He led the Miami Heat to an NBA title playing alongside Shaquille O'Neal. He won an Eastern Conference Championship while playing with Lebron James and Chris Bosh. He's an Olympic champion as well. At the 2008 Summer Olympics, Wade helped the U.S. men's basketball team capture the gold medal in Beijing, China.

Yet Dwyane may be an even greater champion when he's away from the basketball court. Some of the best work he's done hasn't been shooting a basketball—it has been helping kids improve their lives.

Dwyane plays basketball with some kids in Miami.

At the 2008 Olympics, Dwyane was the U.S. team's leading scorer, averaging 16 points a game. In America's 118–107 win over Spain in the gold-medal game, Dwyane led all scorers with 27 points.

Dwyane with his gold medal

The Dwyane File

Dwyane is a basketball hero on and off the court. Here are some highlights.

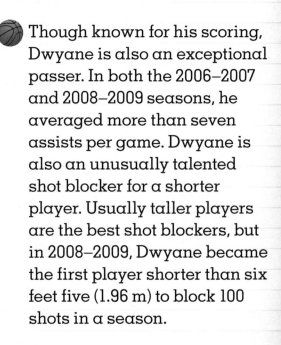

- In 2008–2009, Dwyane averaged 30.2 points a game, leading the entire NBA in scoring. He has averaged more than 25 points a game for his entire career and hit a career high of 55 points in a game against the New York Knicks on April 12, 2009.

- As a child growing up in Chicago, Dwyane was a Chicago Bulls fan who idolized the great Michael Jordan.

- Though known for his scoring, Dwyane is also an exceptional passer. In both the 2006–2007 and 2008–2009 seasons, he averaged more than seven assists per game. Dwyane is also an unusually talented shot blocker for a shorter player. Usually taller players are the best shot blockers, but in 2008–2009, Dwyane became the first player shorter than six feet five (1.96 m) to block 100 shots in a season.

Glossary

center (SEN-tur) one of the standard positions on a basketball team, usually played by the tallest player

charity (CHA-ruh-tee) a group that tries to help people in need

clutch (KLUHCH) able to come up with great plays at very important moments in a game

comeback (KUHM-bak) when one team comes back from being far behind in the game to eventually win

draft (DRAFT) an event in which professional teams take turns choosing college players to play for them

drives (DRIVEZ) rapid moves toward the basket while dribbling the ball

Eastern Conference (EES-turn KON-fur-*uhnss*) one of two 15-team divisions making up the NBA

Final Four (FYE-nuhl FOR) the semifinals of the NCAA college basketball championships; the stage of the basketball tournament where only four teams remain in competition

fouled (FOWLD) hit or interfered with in a manner that is against the rules

four-point play (FOR-point PLAY) a play in which a player hits a three-point shot, is fouled, and then hits a free throw for a total of four points

free throw line (FREE THROH LINE) the line where a player stands to attempt foul shots

guard (GARD) one of the standard positions on a basketball team; a team's two guards are usually the shortest players—they are responsible for handling the basketball and taking longer distance shots.

impact (IM-pakt) the effect someone or something has on something else

lane (LAYN) the painted area beneath the basket between the free throw line and the baseline

layup (LAY-uhp) a shot taken near the basket, usually by playing the ball off the backboard

playoffs (PLAY-awfs) a series of games played to determine which teams will play in a championship

runner (RUN-ur) a high, arching basketball shot taken while the player is running and which is released very quickly with one hand

scholarship (SKOL-ur-ship) money given to a person so that he or she can attend school

23

Bibliography

Jackson, Scoop. "The Responsibility of Being Dwyane Wade." ESPN.com (April 24, 2007).

Lieber, Jill. "Heat Star Wade-ing into Special Territory." *USA Today* (February 17, 2005).

"Wade's World." *Sports Illustrated for Kids* (November 2005).

The Chicago Tribune

Read More

DiPrimio, Pete. *Dwyane Wade (NBA Miami Heat).* Childs, MD: Mitchell Lane (2011).

Gitlin, Marty. *Miami Heat (Inside the NBA).* Edina, MN: ABDO (2012).

Glaser, Jason. *Dwyane Wade.* Pleasantville, NY: Gareth Stevens (2012).

Learn More Online

To learn more about Dwyane Wade and the Miami Heat, visit
www.bearportpublishing.com/BasketballHeroes

Index